Mom, Tell Me Your Story

A Mother's Guided Journal and Memory Keepsake Book

This journal belongs to :

From Your Child :

Paperback ISBN: 978-1-961443-06-8

Published by Harbour House Publishing Press

Printed in the United States of America
Cover design by Victor Oj
Editor and Illustrator: Elsie Bloomfield

Dedicated to my Sons

Valen, vishal & Videl

table of content

introduction

This journal is designed specifically for Mothers of all kinds, whether biological or non-biological, to capture and preserve the significant moments that have shaped your life.

Mom, Tell Me Your Story™

----Mom ----

It's time to write the story of your life with this guided journal.

It's designed to be filled out with an erasable pen or pencil, whichever you prefer.

As you work through the prompts in this journal, you will have the opportunity to record all the important phases of your life, from childhood to elderhood.

You will be able to reflect on your relationships, your achievements, and the challenges you faced. And as you do so, you will be creating a legacy for your grandchildren and future generations to treasure.

In addition to the prompts provided, this journal also includes special pages where you can document your bucket lists, your travels, your hobbies and interests, birthdays, special milestones, memories, and more.

We hope this journal will be a source of joy and fulfillment as you document your life story. Let's get writing!

getting the most out of this journal

welcome to this guided journal! It's important to remember that there are no strict rules or guidelines for using this book. **The format is flexible, allowing you to tackle the questions in any order you choose.** Whether you prefer to skip around or work through them in order, the choice is yours.

As you respond to each question, there is no right or wrong way to answer. You may choose to skip certain questions or replace them with additional ones available on our website. It's important to write freely and record whatever comes to mind and heart without overthinking or holding back. The best answers are the ones that come straight from the heart, without worrying about perfection or formality.

Take your time with answering the questions. As there are many of them, you may want to complete the book over multiple sessions, dedicating some time each day over a period of weeks or months. You can also enlist the help of a family member to ask you the questions out loud and record your answers on video or audio.

HINT:

- When telling your story, use specific details such as first and last names, exact dates, locations, and brand names.
- Describing things like "mist-green 1945 Cadillac" instead of "...Dad's Car" and "... red roses" instead of "flowers" helps make your story more vivid.
- Also, be precise, such as "...Schrafft's on seventh Street, downtown," instead of "...at Schrafft's." This approach will bring your story to life and make it more engaging.

If you need more space to answer a question, you can utilize the extra notes pages at the end of each section or include memorable photos. Remember to go easy on yourself and enjoy the process of reflecting on your life experiences.

...my details, time capsule and family tree.

chapter 1:
the family tree

This chapter is dedicated to the Family Tree, a beautiful tapestry that weaves together the stories, memories, and love that my roots, and I can't think of a better person than you, My Mom, to guide me on this journey of discovery.

Understanding our family tree is essential for me to build a deeper connection with our past, our ancestors, and our heritage. By sharing your stories and experiences, you are allowing me to preserve the legacy of the generations that came before us. This exercise will not only strengthen our bond with you but will also foster a sense of belonging and identity within us.

Through your words, I want to feel the emotions, the struggles, the joys, and the triumphs that you and our ancestors have experienced.

This will give me a greater appreciation for who we are and where we come from. It will also enable me to carry forward the values and traditions that have shaped our family's history.

By taking the time to reflect on and share these stories with me, you are creating a treasure trove of memories and wisdom that I can cherish forever. This will not only give me a sense of pride in our family history but also inspire me to carry on the values and traditions that you and our ancestors have passed down through the generations.

Thank you, Mom, for embarking on this emotional and meaningful journey with me. I can't wait to learn more about our Family Tree and grow even closer to you in the process.

MY DETAILS

Full Name

Place of Birth

Eye Color

Hair Color

Height

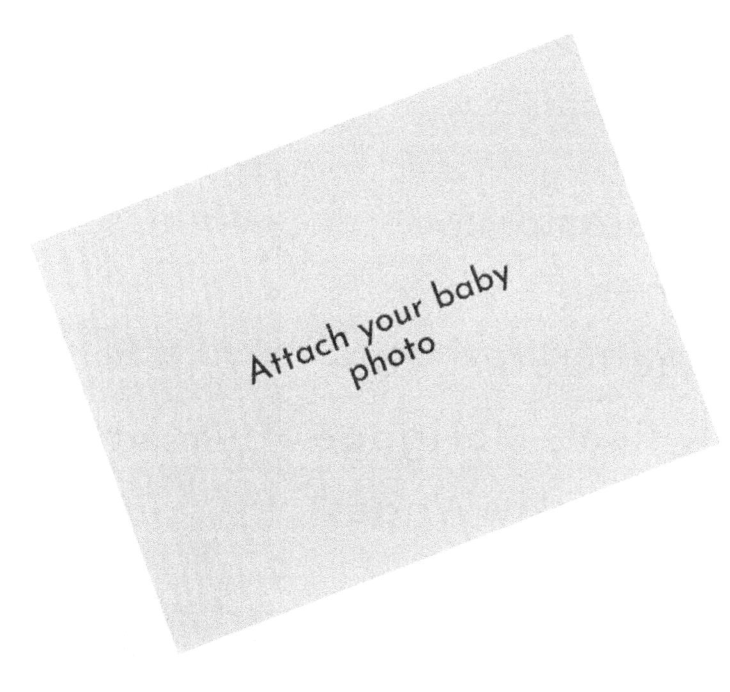

time capsule

TODAY'S DATE ....

The Price of...

Gallon of Milk	
Gallon of Gasoline	
Movie Ticket	
Landline Telephone	
Pair of Jeans	
Vinyl Music Album	
Loaf of Bread	
Movie Rental (VHS)	
Fast-Food Meal	
New Car	
Magazine	
Postage Stamp	
Newspaper	
Mortgage Interest Rate	
Monthly Rent/Mortgage Payment	
Average Weekly Wages	
Average House Rate	

FAMILY TREE

Your Great Grandmother

Your Great Grandfather

Your Great Grandmother

Your Great Grandfather

Your Grandmother

Your Grandfather

Your Father

Your Brothers

You

FAMILY TREE

Your Great Grandmother

Your Great Grandfather

Your Great Grandmother

Your Great Grandfather

Your Grandmother

Your Grandfather

Your Mother

Your Sisters

YOUR FAVOURITE.......

Color

Number

Flower

Animal

Films

Actors

Songs

Musicians

Books

Authors

Seasons

Country

TV Series

Weather

getting to know you more...

Food:

Drink:

Color:

Hobby:

Song:

Show:

Games:

App:

City:

Country:

...growing up

Chapter 2:
growing up

as your child, I want to know your story - the experiences and emotions that shaped the incredible person we call our mother. This guided journal session aims to help you delve into your memories, revisiting your childhood and adolescence. By sharing your story, you not only strengthen the bond between us, but also give us a deeper understanding of who you are and the life you've lived.

In this chapter, we'll focus on "Growing Up." This is the beginning of your journey, where the foundations of your character were laid. We encourage you to share your most vivid memories, emotions, and experiences from this time in your life.

It's important for me to hear your story, to understand the challenges you faced and the lessons you learned, as it provides me with a connection to our family history and the values that have been passed down to us.

Sharing your story of growing up is a beautiful way for us to better understand the incredible woman you are. It's a chance for us to learn about the experiences that shaped your life, the emotions you felt, and the relationships that nurtured and supported you. Your story is a treasure trove of wisdom, and we are eager to learn from your journey.

this or that

extravert	introvert
books	movies
art	sport
burger	pizza
juice	soda
dark	light
academia	academia
dogs	cats

Growing Up

When and where were you born?

Where did you grow up?

Growing Up

What was it like?

How would you describe yourself as a child? Were you happy?

Growing Up

What is one of your best memories of childhood? Worst?

Did you have a nickname? How'd you get it?

Growing Up

Do you have any favorite stories from your childhood?

When you were a child, what did you want to be when you grew up?

Other Things

Other Things

...family heritage

this or that

Coffee	Tea
Chesee Cake	Cupcake
Mounth	Beach
Pizza	Burger
Paris	Hawai
Flat Shoes	Casual Shoes
Hot	Ice
Cooking	Reading
Music	Karaoke

Tell it All Books

Chapter 3:
Family Heritage

We are about to embark on a heartfelt journey together, as we delve into our family heritage. This chapter is an invitation for you to share your story, your experiences, and the legacy of our family with your children. By answering these questions, you are helping us understand our roots, appreciate our ancestry, and strengthen our connection to you.

Family heritage is the tapestry woven from generations of love, sacrifice, and wisdom. Each thread holds memories, stories, and traditions that create a rich tapestry of who we are. As your children, we want to cherish and preserve this precious legacy. We believe that your insights will not only deepen our understanding of our family history but also instill a sense of pride and belonging that will last a lifetime.

This exercise is essential because, through your eyes, we can discover the origins of our family values and traditions. We can learn about the resilience and determination of our ancestors, who overcame adversity to create the life we know today. By understanding the people who came before us, we can better appreciate the struggles and triumphs that have shaped our family.

In sharing your story, you are also creating a lasting gift for future generations. Your words will serve as a bridge, connecting the past with the present and the future. As we grow older, we will carry your stories with us, passing them down to our children and grandchildren, ensuring that our family heritage remains alive and vibrant.

As you answer the questions in this chapter, we encourage you to be open, honest, and vulnerable, as your words will become a cherished treasure for us.

Family

Who were your parents? ....

What were your parents like? ....

Family

How was your relationship with your parents?

Do you have any siblings? What were they like growing up?

Family

Who were your favorite relatives? ....

....

....

....

....

....

....

....

Do you remember any of the stories your grandparents used to tell you? ....

....

....

....

....

....

....

....

....

....

....

....

....

Family

How did you and grandma/grandpa meet? ....

Do you remember any songs that you used to sing to your children? ....

Family

Were your grandparents well-behaved? ....

What were your parents like? ....

What were your grandparents like? ....

FAMILY HERITAGE

Where are your parents' families from?

Have you ever been there? What was that experience like?

FAMILY HERITAGE

What traditions have been passed down in your family?

Do you remember any traditional story about your family?

FAMILY HERITAGE

What are the classic family stories? Jokes? Songs?

Do you remember any traditional story about your family?

Other Things

Other Things

...career

Tell it All Books

Chapter 4:
career

In this chapter, we want to explore and understand your professional journey, which has played an essential role in shaping who you are today. Your career is not only about the work you've done; it's a reflection of your dedication, strength, resilience, and growth. By sharing your career story, you are allowing us to see how your experiences have enriched your life and the lives of those around you.

This exercise is crucial for both your children and you because it serves as a bridge between generations. As your children, we are eager to learn from your wisdom and draw inspiration from your accomplishments. We want to know how you navigated the challenges and celebrated the triumphs that accompanied your professional life.

Moreover, we wish to understand the values that guided your decisions, so we can apply them to our own lives.

Your career story also offers you the opportunity to reflect on your journey, appreciate the milestones you've reached, and be proud of your achievements. By documenting your experiences, you can recognize the impact you've had and celebrate your unique contributions. Additionally, this exercise serves as a way to preserve your legacy and pass on valuable life lessons to future generations.

We encourage you to be open, candid, and emotionally connected as you respond to these questions. Your insights will not only bring us closer together but also help us understand and appreciate the beautiful tapestry of your life. Thank you, Mom, for taking the time to share your story with us. We can't wait to learn more about the remarkable woman you are.

This or That

WEEKEND ACTIVITIES

Read books	Listen to a podcast
Cook food	Order in
Wake up early	Wake up late
Sleep early	Sleep late
Alone time	Family time
Learn a new dish	Learn a new skill
Do chores	Declutter
Workout	Relax
Movie marathon	TV series binge watching

School

Did you enjoy school?

What kind of student were you?

What would you do for fun?

School

How would your classmates remember you?

Are you still friends with anyone from that time in your life?

What are your best memories of grade school/high school/college/graduate school?

School

Worst memories?

Was there a teacher or teachers who had a particularly strong influence on your life? Tell me about them.

Career

Describe the work that you do. ....

Tell me about how you got into your line of work. ....

Career

Do you like your job?

What did you think you were going to be when you grew up?

Career

What did you want to be when you grew up? ....

What lessons has your work life taught you? ....

Career

If you could do anything now, what would you do? Why?

Do you plan on retiring? If so, when? How do you feel about it?

Career

Do you have any favorite stories from your work life?

Other Things

Other Things

...love and relationship

this or that

Forest	Mountain
America	Europe
Summer	Winter
Pack Light	Overpack
Local food	Fancy reSto
Glamping	Camping
Hotel	Airbnb
Small town	City life

Chapter 5:
love and relationship

As your children, we are eager to learn about your story, to better understand your wisdom, your heartache, and your growth. This exercise is not only a way for us to connect with you on a deeper level, but also for you to reflect on the richness of your emotional experiences.

Your experiences with love and relationships help us understand the person you were before becoming our mother. They offer insights into the decisions you've made, the joys and challenges you've faced, and the values you've developed. By sharing your story, you create a lasting legacy for us to cherish and learn from as we navigate our own journeys in love and relationships.

a lot of deep and emotional/personal questions will be asked in this section.

As you answer these questions, we encourage you to be open, vulnerable, and honest. We understand that some memories may be difficult to revisit, but know that sharing them with us will only deepen our love and appreciation for you. Through this exercise, we hope to connect with you on a deeper level, grow together as a family, and cherish the beautiful story that is your life.

Friendships

Who Was you best friend? ....

....

....

....

....

....

....

....

....

What was your first memory of your best friend ....

....

....

....

....

....

....

....

....

....

....

....

Friendships

What things makes such good friends?

How would you describe your friends?

Friendships

How would you describe yourself to your friends?

What is the presents situation of friendships

How frequently do you communicate with your friends?

Love & Relationships

Do you have a love of your life?

When did you first fall in love?

Can you tell me about your first kiss?

Love & Relationships

What was your first serious relationship?

Do you ever think about previous lovers?

What lessons have you learned from your relationships?

Love & Relationships

Who were the "ones that got away" in your life?

What was the hardest break up you've ever experienced?

Do you remember the best date you ever went on?

Marriage & Partnership

How did you meet your spouse/partner? ....

....

....

....

....

....

....

....

....

How did you know they were "the one"? ....

....

....

....

....

....

How did you propose? ....

....

....

....

....

....

Marriage & Partnership

What were the best times?

The most difficult times?

Marriage & Partnership

What advice do you have for young couples?

Do you have any favorite stories from your marriage or about your partner?

Other Things

Other Things

...parenting

this or that

sunrise	sunset
sweet	savory
sun	moon
early bird	night owl
take a risk	just relax
park	beach
family time	me time
bar	cafe
diy	buy
tv series	movies

Chapter 6: parenting

This chapter is dedicated to exploring the beautiful, challenging, and emotional journey of parenting. By sharing your story with us, your children, you'll be providing us with an invaluable connection to our family history and your personal experiences as our mother. This exercise is not only a precious gift for us, but it also offers you the opportunity to reflect on your parenting journey, the triumphs and tribulations, and the deep emotions that have shaped who you are today.

Your parenting story is essential for several reasons:

1. Understanding our roots: As your children, we desire to know where we come from and how our upbringing has shaped us.
2. Building empathy and connection: By giving us insights into your emotional journey as a parent, we can better appreciate your sacrifices, your dedication, and your love.

3. Learning from your wisdom: Your experiences offer us invaluable lessons about life, relationships, and parenting.

4 Self-reflection and healing: This process of self-discovery can be therapeutic and empowering, allowing you to heal from past experiences and grow as a person.

In this chapter, we encourage you to delve deep into your emotions, recall the moments that have shaped you as a parent, and be open and honest with us. Share the joys, the fears, the laughter, and the tears that have accompanied your journey. We want to know your proudest moments, your struggles, and the lessons you've learned along the way.

As you embark on this emotional exploration, remember that there's no right or wrong way to tell your story. It's your journey, your emotions, and your truth.

Parenting

When did you first find out that you'd be a parent? How did you feel?

Did you always know you wanted to be a parent?

Parenting

Can you describe the moment when you saw your child for the first time?

How has being a parent changed you?

Parenting

What have you learned about yourself from being a parent?

What are your dreams for your children?

Parenting

Do you remember when your last child left home for good?

Do you have any favorite stories about your kids?

Other Things

Other Things

...health & religion

Chapter 7:
Health

This chapter is all about your journey through health, a deeply personal and emotional topic that holds incredible significance for your children. They want to understand your story, empathize with your experiences, and learn valuable lessons from your challenges and triumphs.

As your children embark on their own life journeys, gaining insights into your health history is crucial to understanding the genetic and lifestyle factors that may impact their well-being. By sharing your story, you're giving them the gift of knowledge, enabling them to make informed decisions about their own health.

By delving into your past, present, and future health, you'll be providing a comprehensive portrait of the woman they know and love. Your narrative will touch on both physical and emotional aspects of your health, painting a vivid picture of your resilience and strength.

This exercise is important for your children because:

1.Connection

2.Understanding

3.Growth

4.Wisdom

5.Legacy

In this chapter, you'll be answering a series of questions that will prompt you to delve into your health experiences. You'll be asked to share your memories, emotions, and insights, painting a rich portrait of your health journey for your children.

As you embark on this exercise, know that your children will cherish every word, drawing strength and inspiration from your experiences. This is an opportunity to create a lasting legacy, one that will deepen your connection and shape their lives for years to come.

this or that

Sport Edition

Aquatic	Golf
Archery	Gymnastics
Badminton	Football
Basketball	Pentathlon
Boxing	Table tennis
Taekwondo	Bicycle
Weightlifting	Volleyball
Long jump	Tennis

Religion

What is your religion? ....

....

....

....

Can you tell me about your religious beliefs/spiritual beliefs?..............................

....

....

....

....

....

....

....

....

....

....

....

....

....

....

....

....

Religion

How did you come to your faith?

How has your faith evolved over time?

Religion

What was the most profound spiritual moment of your life? ....

Do you believe in God? ....

Religion

How have you experienced God (or a Higher Power) in your life?

Do you believe in the after-life? What do you think it will be like?

Serious Illness

Can you tell me about your illness?

Do you think about dying? Are you scared?

Serious Illness

Has this illness changed you?

What have you learned?

Other Things

Other Things

...Leisure/ Passion/ travelling

this or that

Fashion Edition

Shoe	Shirt
Culottes	Hat
Skirt	Jacket
Jeans	Hoodie
Long Dress	Sweater
pajamas	Blouse
Tunic	Flatshoes
Blouse	Headband

Chapter 8: Travelling/leisure/passion

In this chapter of our guided journal, we invite you to share your stories of travel and exploration. Travel has a unique way of broadening our horizons, teaching us about different cultures and people, and shaping our outlook on life.

As your children, we would be honored to learn about the journeys that have had a profound impact on your life, both physically and emotionally.
By sharing your travel experiences, you give us a chance to relive those moments with you, to understand the emotions you felt, and to learn from the wisdom you gained.

This exercise will not only help us connect with you on a deeper level but also serve as a valuable lesson in empathy and understanding for us.

The stories you share will become cherished memories that we can carry with us, and perhaps even pass on to future generations.

In this chapter, we encourage you to share the stories that have touched your heart or made you see the world differently. Tell us about the places you visited, the people you met, and the experiences that made a lasting impression on you.

Describe the sights, sounds, and smells that you encountered, and don't shy away from sharing the challenges you faced and the emotions you experienced.
As you recount your travels, please consider the following questions:

1.What inspired you to embark on your most memorable journey?
2.How did this trip change your perspective on life, people, or the world?
3.Can you share a particular moment or encounter that moved you deeply?
4.What challenges did you face during your travels, and how did you overcome them?
5.How have your travels shaped your relationships, values, and beliefs?

By answering these questions, you will help us discover the incredible experiences that have shaped your life. Your stories will inspire us to embark on our own journeys, learn from other cultures, and appreciate the beauty of our world.

So, dear Mom, let us embark on this journey together and explore the fascinating tapestry of your life's travels.

Favorite Things

What is your favorite color?

What is your favorite season?

Favorite Things

What is your favorite car to drive? ....

What is your favorite book? ....

Favorite Things

What is your favorite moment in history? ....

What is your favorite perfume/cologne scent? ....

Traveling

What is your favorite country to travel to? ....

....

....

....

....

....

....

....

....

....

What is your favorite continent to travel to? ....

....

....

....

....

....

....

....

....

....

....

Traveling

What is your favorite vacation that you have ever been on?

What is your favorite picture taken on vacation?

Traveling

Who is your favorite person to travel with?

What is your favorite thing to bring with you when traveling?

Traveling

What is your favorite food that you have had while on vacation?

Other Things

Other Things

...note to loved ones

this or that

Cat person	Dog person
Jeans	Cullotes
Bright color	Neutral color
Music	Movie
Text	Phone call
Early bird	Night owl
Work out	Watch tv
Staying in	Going out

Note to Loved Ones

Note to Loved Ones

Note to Loved Ones

Note to Loved Ones

Note to Loved Ones

Note to Loved Ones

conclusion

Mom, as we reach the conclusion of this guided journal session, we want to take a moment to express our deepest gratitude for your willingness to embark on this journey with us. We know that it might not have been easy to delve into the various chapters of your life, but your courage and openness will create a lasting keepsake for us to cherish for years to come.

We understand that some memories and emotions may be difficult to share, but please remember that your story, in its entirety, is what makes you the incredible, strong, and loving mother we know and admire. We encourage you to embrace vulnerability and not to hold back, as this will only strengthen our bond and deepen our understanding of who you truly are.

Each chapter of your life has shaped you into the person you are today, and by sharing these experiences with us, you're providing us with the unique opportunity to walk alongside you on your journey. Your story will serve as a beacon of inspiration, wisdom, and love for us and future generations.

As we look back on this guided journal session, may it serve as a constant reminder of the love, strength, and resilience that courses through our family. Let your words be a testament to your incredible journey and a source of comfort, guidance, and connection for us all.

Thank you, Mom, for gifting us with this precious keepsake. We are truly honored to learn from you and to share in the legacy you've created.

Notes

Notes

Notes

Notes

GET THIS BOOK
FREE NOW

Scan This Code
or Visit >>

bit.ly/Einkling

Made in United States
North Haven, CT
20 December 2023